A MYRIAD OF
MYSTERIES

A MYRIAD OF
MYSTERIES

...a journey into the unknown

JAMES SANDERSON

London

A Myriad of Mysteries

The book information is catalogued as follows;
Author Name(s): James Sanderson
Title: A Myriad of Mysteries
Description; First Edition

1st Edition, 2021

Book design by Leah Kent
Cover design by Jonathan Benjamin

ISBN: 978-1-914447-12-9 (ebook)
ISBN: 978-1-914447-11-2 paperback)

Published by That Guy's House
www.ThatGuysHouse.com

*This book is dedicated to my Mother
Isabelle Brenda or 'Min' 1917-2019 who I had the
privilege to know and her wonderful friend and
Carer in the latter years of her life, Gabby.*

Contents

Introduction

This last year in 2020, I stayed for a while somewhere where there was a ghost. This was completely outside my sphere of belief or understanding, but there it was, almost every night, a knock on the bedroom door, sometimes faintly or very loudly or even on one occasion rattling the door handle. Eventually, the ghost left us, but this experience stretched my thinking completely.

Now this book is not about the supernatural, but it is about things that are difficult or impossible to understand. We can resist it or embrace it, but the reality is that we simply do not know or understand everything and that, I would suggest, is a good place to be.

Mysteries stretch our minds to think differently and to contemplate the unknown. They are fascinating and troubling at the same time. It is like a workout for the mind because as we prepare a place for the unknown, we can ask ourselves new questions and contemplate new ideas that we can begin to formulate and even comprehend.

Unsolved crimes, unexplained questions, disappearances and strange occurrences are all here.

My hope is that as you read these things, you will begin to think new things and contemplate new ideas for yourself and your life and perhaps even for the people around you and the wider world beyond.

I hope you will consider it as if you are embarking on a journey here for yourself as you read these things, to wind back what you know to perhaps 50% of what you are prepared to accept and leave the rest for the unknown.

When I was a small boy, my parents often used to take me sailing, and it was forever a fascination for me as we used to untie the mooring ropes and leave the land to set sail, and that is what this book is all about, leaving what we know.

Scientists say that 96% of the Universe we do not understand and so not knowing is a very good thing because there is a lot more to be known.

Let the journey begin!

Mysteries stretch our minds
to think differently and to
contemplate the unknown.

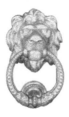

1. Archaeological Finds

"An Archeologist is the best husband a woman can have. The older she gets, the more interested he is in her."

-Agatha Christie

The Antikythera Mechanism

In 1900, a crew of sponge divers discovered an ancient shipwreck off the coast of Antikythera in Greece. From 1900 onward, various artefacts and treasures were brought up from this wreck, a Roman cargo ship that had sunk in the first century BC on the way from Rome to Asia. The items retrieved from the wreck were taken to the National Museum for Archaeology in Athens. In 1902, one team member working to clean and catalogue the treasures noticed what seemed to be a gear embedded in a rock. He assumed it to have been some form of ancient clock, but nothing further was deduced. No one paid the device much attention until 1951, when a British science historian named Derek J de Solla Price became interested in it. He and Charalampos Karakalos, a Greek nuclear physicist, took x-rays of the known 82 fragments of the Mechanism in 1971, and in 1974 they published an extensive report on their findings. Further dive expeditions to look for more pieces of the Mechanism began in 2014.

The Antikythera Mechanism is thought to be the world's first analogue computer. Inscriptions on the device have led researchers to conclude that it was used to predict the movements of the stars and planets as well as lunar and solar eclipses. The device would have reflected the geocentric view of the universe held at the time – meaning the belief that the Earth was at the centre of the universe. There has been speculation about the date of its origin, ranging from 65 BC to as far back as 200 BC, and attempted models of the device have been created over the years, as scientists try to figure out how the device would have worked and what it would have looked like.

In March 2021, researchers at the University of London (UCL) announced they would attempt to recreate the device. Using a mathematical method devised by the Greek philosopher Parmenides, the team has worked out a way to recreate the gear arrangements to allow the device to move in the way it would have been designed, with the Earth at the centre; they intend to recreate it using only tools and methods that would have been available at the time it was built. A statement from the UCL says, "Ours is the first model that conforms to all the physical evidence and matches the descriptions in the scientific inscriptions engraved on the Mechanism itself. The Sun, Moon and planets are displayed in an impressive tour de force of ancient Greek brilliance."

Qin Shi Huang's tomb/ Mausoleum of the First Qin Emperor

In 1974, farmers in Xiyang made an interesting discovery while drilling for a well: they found bronze arrowheads and pieces of terracotta. When they took these items to sell at the local cultural centre, they didn't realise they had discovered one of the most incredible archaeological finds of the 20th century.

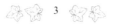

An astounding underground complex, more like an arrangement of cities, over 35 square miles in size, lay beneath their feet. This complex is the tomb of the First Emperor, Emperor Qin Shi Huang (259 BC – 210 BC), and contains an entire army of terracotta soldiers, complete with horses, chariots, and weapons. The army was crafted to guard the Emperor in the afterlife; however, it remains to be discovered where precisely the Emperor himself is buried or what treasures might have been buried with him. A pyramid-shaped tomb lies north of where the army was found, but no one has entered it yet.

This tomb is the most opulent and extensive ever constructed in China, if not the entire world. The soldiers' faces are all unique and individually carved, and they are arranged in military formation, divided into units. The complex also contains an advanced drainage system, an exotic zoo, stables, and countless other artefacts. Much remains to be discovered in the Mausoleum of the First Emperor; however, dangerous mercury levels, as well as concern for the preservation of the site, has prevented further exploration of the tomb of the Emperor himself.

Ancient Animal Traps

In the early 20th century, pilots discovered what looked like low stone walls crisscrossing the deserts of Jordan, Egypt, and Israel. These walls were nicknamed 'kites' by scientists, based on their appearance from the air, and went on for about 40 miles. They date back to around 300 BC but seem to have been abandoned long ago.

Recent studies suggest that the walls served to funnel wild animals into smaller pits, where hunters could quickly kill them. If this is true, it shows that ancient hunters were a bit more clever than we thought!

Shroud of Turin

One of the most hotly debated archaeological finds is the Shroud of Turin, believed by many to be the burial cloth of Jesus Christ himself. The Shroud itself bears traces of blood and the imprint of a man's body – but is that man Jesus? The Catholic Church's records show the Shroud's existence being discovered in France in AD 1353, yet the legend goes back a bit further, all the way to AD 30 or 33 when Jesus was crucified. Legend has it that the Shroud was transported from Judea, then on to Turkey and later to Constantinople. When crusaders in AD 1204 raided Constantinople, the Shroud was moved to Athens, where it was allegedly held until AD 1225.

Finally, in the 1980s, three small pieces of cloth from the Shroud were sent off for radiocarbon date testing at three different facilities. All three tests showed the fabric was created between 1260 and 1390 AD, thus making it a medieval forgery. Of course, critics of this research state that the researchers tested newer parts of the Shroud that were stitched together centuries after Jesus' death, thus making the Shroud seem more contemporary than it actually is. Despite the science, the faith of many remains strong, and the Shroud of Turin is viewed as a holy relic today.

King Tut's Death

One of the most famous and infamous archaeological finds of the 20th century, King Tutankhamun's tomb, has been shrouded in mystery and legend since its discovery in 1922. While everyone has heard of the 'pharaoh's curse' who befalls anyone who dares to venture into the tomb, one of the bigger mysteries concerns the actual death of the pharaoh. It is speculated that the boy king died from an infection or a chariot accident – an untimely death, at any rate. It has been supposed that his burial may have been rushed, based on what appears to be a poorly executed job of embalming his royal corpse. His mummy seems to have caught fire after the tomb was sealed, most likely due to the linen wrapping his body being soaked in flammable embalming fluids, which may have reacted with the oxygen in the air. The result was that the mummy was essentially cooked at about 200 degrees Celsius. Not exactly the ideal royal send-off. This hasty and somewhat disastrous burial suggests the tomb may have been intended for someone else, which leads to the belief that other mummies may be discovered in the tomb.

The *Kofun* Tombs

Japan has its own version of the pyramids: the *kofun* ('old tombs'), built by hundreds of workers to house the remains of great kings. The basic design came from Korea, another import from the mainland to Japan, like rice agriculture and Buddhism.

Kofun first started appearing across Japan around AD 250; they were small to start, just simple chambers built into the ground with a structure over the top to create a mound. Later on, in the fifth century, *kofun* could be hundreds of metres across and rather grand affairs. The *kofun* that have been excavated so far have contained wooden coffins, bronze mirrors, masterfully crafted swords, iron armour, and other precious objects. The slopes of the mounds outside would be decorated with terracotta figurines as boundary markers with intricate designs, such as boats, birds, dancers, female shaman, warriors, and horses.

The grandest of all *kofun* is the *Daisen kofun*, located in Osaka. This *kofun* was constructed in the fifth century and contains three moats, is nearly half a kilometre long, 300 metres wide and 30 metres high! Its splendour and keyhole shape can only truly be appreciated from the air, and it's guaranteed that someone rather extraordinary lies beneath.

But alas, we shall never know who lies within the *Daisen kofun*, as in Japan, it's forbidden to excavate a *kofun* over a specific size or in the shape of a keyhole: such *kofun* were created for divine emperors, and to excavate them would be considered a sacrilege. However, critics suggest that the real reason the tombs are off-limits is that there is the potential to find something inside that could call into question the history of the world's oldest monarchy, which is a risk the Imperial Household Agency doesn't want to take.

Gobekli Tepe

It has long been thought that from about 8000 BC, humans first settled into permanent towns, then set up farms and agriculture, and then built temples – in that order. However, a remarkable archaeological discovery in 1994 turned that theory on its head.

What appeared to be the world's oldest place of worship was discovered in Gobekli Tepe, in a rural part of Turkey, causing historians to question the evolution of civilisation. Dating back to the tenth millennium BC, the site contains multiple rings of massive stone pillars carved with animals. It also appeared that semi-nomadic hunters had built the site centuries before the advent of agriculture, leading experts to wonder if perhaps building temples like this one led to settlement rather than the other way around.

The Copper Scroll Treasure

An ancient copper scroll discovered alongside the Dead Sea Scrolls in 1952 at the site of Qumran might contain information regarding a fantastic treasure of silver and gold, but no one is sure if it exists or where it can be found. The scroll dates back to 2,000 years ago when Rome occupied the area and is believed to describe a treasure that the locals hid to keep it out of Roman hands.

Whether this treasure is real, and if so, where it might be, remain mysteries to this day.

The Hobbits

No, not the ones in the Shire. In 2003, scientists on the remote Indonesian island of Flores discovered the bones of the small hominin (human ancestor), now known as *Homo floresiens*. The bones were of a three and a half foot tall, 30-year-old adult female, and the scientists quickly nicknamed her 'The Hobbit'.

Researchers thought at first that she was a human with microcephalia, a condition characterised by short height and a small head. However, further discoveries of similarly sized skeletons suggest that *H. floresiens* was, in fact, its own species, not just a tiny human.

Where 'The Hobbit' fits in with our family tree has yet to be discovered.

The Cochno Stone

In Glasgow, Scotland, archaeologists excavated a massive 5,000-year-old stone slab in 2016 – and then buried it again, and not for the first time. The so-called Cochno Stone was first unearthed in 1887, but by 1965 it had been vandalised with graffiti and damaged by the elements. Hence, a team of archaeologists decided to rebury it for protection. It was briefly re-excavated in 2016 to allow the use of modern-day surveying and photography to record the artwork present on the stone.

It's this artwork that makes the stone significant – the swirling patterns known as 'cup and ring marks' have been found at prehistoric sites all over the world. It's been suggested that the designs might have something to do with astronomical phenomenon like eclipses; however, current research is being done on the stone to ascertain how prehistorical people may have used it.

Holey Jar

Many holy relics have been discovered throughout the years, but a holey jar is a new phenomenon. This jar was found in a WWII bomb crater outside of London and dates back to Roman Britain. Researchers have speculated that the jar may have been part of a lamp or used as an animal cage for mice or snakes – two very different theories, yet theories are all they have at the moment. The strange-looking jar is currently on display at the Museum of Ontario Archaeology in Canada. Researchers are hoping for further discoveries or information to shed light on what the possible use of the item may have been.

The reality is that
we simply do not know or
understand everything.

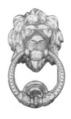

2. History

"Human history in essence
is the history of ideas."

- HG Wells

Oak Island

Legend of a fabulous trove of treasure has swirled around Oak Island for more than two centuries. This island off the coast of Nova Scotia, Canada, is rumoured to hold a cache of buried treasure hidden by the pirate Captain William Kidd (1645-1701). Since his death, many have tried to find this treasure, mounting several expeditions costing millions of dollars. A TV show aired on the History Channel, called 'Curse of Oak Island', following one such expedition.

This supposed treasure has yet to be found.

The Feejee Mermaid

Legends of mermaids have captivated us for centuries. Clever PT Barnum knew this, so it's no wonder he had a 'genuine' mermaid in his American Museum in the early 1840s. The Feejee Mermaid first appeared in the early 19th century, a 3-foot-long, half-humanoid, half-aquatic mummified creature supposedly caught by Japanese sailors off the coast of Fiji. The creature changed hands multiple times for princely sums of money, finally ending up with PT Barnum, who gave it pride of place in his Museum in 1842.

South Pacific fishermen were notorious for creating strange 'creatures' by piecing together fish tails with monkey torsos or similar to impress visitors, who often included wealthy Europeans. These sorts of visitors were eager to have such curiosities to display in their collections back home, and the fishermen were happy to oblige. Even if they knew the objects were fakes, they still wanted to have something fantastical to admire.

The mystery of the Feejee Mermaid doesn't end there – after its time at PT Barnum's American Museum had finished, the Mermaid disappeared. Various copies of the Mermaid have turned up over the years but have always been exposed as fakes. The location of the original Feejee Mermaid remains unknown.

The Dancing Plague

If you happened to be walking down the streets of Strasbourg in 1518, you might have witnessed a strange sight: a crowd of more than 400 people dancing through the town. Not to any music, but simply writhing and frolicking in a sort of frenzy, not stopping for rest, food, or water. This 'dancing plague' was nothing new – a similar situation afflicted the Rhine in 1374. Records from the time state, 'First of all they fell foaming to the ground; then they got up and danced themselves to death.'

No one has ever been able to explain the cause of this phenomenon fully. At the time, it was said to be demonic influence, but recent attempts by historians to diagnose the dancers suggested Sydenham's chorea or chorea minor, a disease characterised by jerking movements in the hands, face, and feet. Other ideas have been proposed, such as types of psychotropic fungus, which can cause hysteria when eaten – similar to what is now thought to have happened in Salem, New England, resulting in the witch trials. Yet another suggestion is mass mental illness, brought on by the stress of the time. It's not too far-fetched to think the stress of living through war, famine, and plague of the time could lead to a sort of mass hysteria.

Whatever the cause, many of the dancers quite literally danced themselves to death, succumbing to exhaustion, dehydration, or starvation. And for now, the cause of the dancing plague remains a mystery.

Why did Chairman Mao's successor flee China?

The world was astonished when on 13 September 1971, the senior Chinese Communist Party leader and army general Lin Biao died when his jet crashed into the Gobi Desert. Lin Biao, leader of the People's Liberation Army, had been the chosen successor to Chairman Mao, the leader since the Communist Revolution in 1949. Biao's skill as a general had helped lead the party to victory during the civil war (1946-1949), and his renown had grown through the sixties and seventies.

However, on 13 September, in the early hours of the day, Lin and his family fled their home and rushed to the jet, which later crashed when it ran out of fuel. As one of Mao's

most trusted colleagues, this behaviour seems out of character. The official story from China was that Lin planned to overthrow the government and was attempting to escape arrest by fleeing to the Soviet Union. However, this explanation doesn't make sense as Lin would not have to have waited long to take power, as Mao was very ill by the early seventies. A theory made in later years was that Jiang Qing, Lin's wife, was opposed to improving relations with the United States, whereas the prime minister at the time was favourable to improving a connection with the States, and this conflict led them to flee before they got caught up in court politics. Another suggestion is that Lin was simply tired of politics by 1971 and sought to escape.

Just to make things more confusing – in recent years, more evidence has come to light that has revealed that the jet was originally heading south, not north, from Beijing, which means the Soviet Union couldn't have been the intended destination. To this day, there is still no conclusive evidence explaining why Lin and his family died trying to flee the country.

What happened to the princes in the Tower?

Following Edward IV's death in April 1483, battle lines were drawn over who would ascend to the throne. On one side were the Woodvilles, young Edward V's mother and relations. On the other side was Edward V's uncle on his father's side, Richard, Duke of Gloucester. As Edward's family was en route to London for the boy's coronation, their convoy was stopped by Gloucester, and three of Edward's companions were arrested.

Elizabeth Woodville, Edward's mother, fled to Westminster Abbey for sanctuary when she heard the news, taking her youngest son, Richard of York, and his five sisters. After the arrests, Edward V continued to his coronation with his uncle, the Duke of Gloucester. Edward was placed in the Tower of London to wait for his crowning, and on 10 May, Gloucester was named Protector. Nothing of interest happened until 13 June, when suddenly Edward IV's close friend William Hastings was seized and beheaded for treason against the Protector. A couple of days later, Gloucester's men surrounded Westminster Abbey and demanded Elizabeth hand over her youngest son, who was then put into the Tower with his brother. The following week, the boys were declared illegitimate, which made Gloucester the legitimate Yorkist heir. He assumed the throne as King Richard III four days later. It is uncertain if he had a hand in the affair or was merely the benefactor of the whole experience.

To add to the mystery, no one knows what became of the two little princes in the Tower. Some sources claim they were 'put to silence', while others claim they survived and were taken away to safety under cover of darkness. Years later, many men came forward, claiming to be the missing

Yorkists, yet no one knows for sure. The mystery continues to fascinate people now, nearly 500 years later.

The Voynich Manuscript

Discovered in 1912, the Voynich manuscript is one of the most talked-about books of the 20th century – which is remarkable as no one can read it. The 250-page book, which dates to the 15th century, is written in some sort of code or unknown alphabet and features illustrations including medicinal herbs, astrology, and astronomy, as well as what appears to be recipes. One series of drawings shows nude females lounging in water, surrounded by systems of pipes – perhaps a description of the benefits of bathing?

Some have theorised that judging by the illustrations, the book may contain alchemical and magical processes, which were being increasingly studied in Europe in the 15th and 16th centuries, but always in secret, as the Church looked down on such practices. This could account for why the book was written in code. Others claim the book is merely a Renaissance-era hoax. Stephen Bax, a professor of linguistics in England, claims to have deciphered part of the manuscript in 2014 and says it is a book about nature. Until the code is fully cracked, no one will know for sure what secrets the manuscript contains.

Where is King Harold buried?

When King Harold Godwinson was defeated by William the Conqueror on 14 October 1066 at the Battle of Hastings, the fate of Anglo-Saxon England was decided. What is undecided is what happened to Harold's body when the battle was over. Some say he was buried at a family manor in Sussex; however, this theory is based on the discovery in 1954 of a grave containing the remains of a well-dressed Anglo-Saxon man in the churchyard. No records exist to suggest a king was buried there, and the bones could have been anyone.

Another source claims Harold was buried at Waltham Abbey in Essex. The Waltham Chronicle states that his body was recovered after the battle by men sent for the purpose, along with his former partner, Edith Swan-Neck, 'who knew the secret marks on the king's body better than others did'. And yet, this Chronicle wasn't written until long after the events, nearly a century later. A new account from another chronicler surfaced in the 13th century claiming Harold had survived the battle and was living out his days as a hermit in Chester.

The final two accounts – the *Carmen de Hastingae Proelio* and the *Gesta Guillelmi* by William of Poitiers – point to Harold being buried on top of a cliff on the Sussex coast, a mocking act, as he was supposedly buried under a sarcastic inscription saying he could continue to guard the shore.

This seems like the most plausible explanation, but no one knows where King Harold's final resting place lies.

Why did the dinosaurs become extinct?

Millions of years ago, over a thousand species of dinosaur roamed the Earth. While theories abound, it has yet to be discovered what wiped the dinosaurs off the face of the planet. One idea called the Alvarez hypothesis (named after Luis and Walter Alvarez, who came up with it) claims that a mountain-sized meteor slammed into Earth 66 million years ago, completely changing the climate as it filled the air with dust, gas, and debris.

Another theory says that rather than the sky, the culprit came from Earth itself, in the form of a volcanic eruption. The discovery of ancient lava flows in India matches up with the end of the Cretaceous period, showing a substantial amount of volcanic activity between 60 and 65 million years ago. The eruption covered 200,000 square miles with layers of volcanic rock that are as much as 6,000 feet thick in places. An explosion of this magnitude would have drastically changed Earth's climate and filled the atmosphere with gases.

Scientists also wonder if perhaps both causes are to blame – that the dinosaurs were the victims of a double-whammy, both from above and below. This debate will most likely continue for years, but the research is an important reminder of the effects of drastic climate change on life on Earth.

Cleopatra's Tomb

Known for her beauty, intelligence, and romantic relationships, Cleopatra remains a mystery as regards her final resting place. When Octavian, their former ally, defeated Cleopatra and Antony in 31 BC at the Battle of Actium, they chose to commit suicide. Plutarch (AD 45-120) describes how the pair were buried together at a 'lofty and beautiful' monument, a site near the temple of the Egyptian goddess Isis. However, the exact location of this tomb remains a mystery. One hopes that if it is ever found, it hasn't fallen prey to grave robbers, which were unfortunately common in ancient times.

**Scientists say that
96% of the Universe
we do not understand.**

3. Wondrous World

"The World is full of wonderful things you haven't seen yet. Don't ever give up on the chance of seeing them."

- JK Rowling

Las Bolas ('The Balls') of Costa Rica

In the Diquis Delta of southern Costa Rica, ancient, giant stone spheres can be found scattered around the landscape. The spheres, dating as far back as 600 AD, are known locally as 'Las Bolas' ('the balls') and are made from a rock formed from molten magma. Their smooth, spherical shape was likely created by using smaller stones to carve them.

A Pre-Columbian civilisation allegedly created these monuments, and it has been speculated that they were used for astronomy or to point the way to significant places. However, no one knows for sure, as the Chibchan people who originally lived in the area and across other parts of Central America vanished with the Spanish conquest. Sadly, the purpose of Las Bolas disappeared too.

Stonehenge

One of the most recognisable monuments in the world and one of the UK's top tourist destinations, Stonehenge has long mystified and befuddled people from all over the globe. How the massive stones were moved and put into place and why such a thing was done at all are questions that have confounded us for ages. And there's far more to Stonehenge than meets the eye – new excavations and underground imaging has revealed that Stonehenge was part of a network of structures of burial mounds and settlements. Discovery of a possible 'Super-Henge' in the area led researchers to look at the whole place differently – as possibly a sacred landscape used in religious or ceremonial processions.

According to discoveries by the Stonehenge Riverside Project, Stonehenge was built in two stages: the inner circle, ditch, and bank were constructed first, over 4,500 years ago, then the iconic outer ring was added around 500 years later. The bluestones used for the inner circle came from the Preseli Hills in Wales, quite a distance away and home to its own prehistoric monuments. The larger stones for the outer ring are said to come from about twenty miles away at the location of another significant site: Avebury. The lesser-known stone circle at Avebury is the largest in the world. The choice of places for the stones suggests that there may have been a link between these sites.

One of the biggest mysteries about Stonehenge is how the massive stones were transported and how they were erected once they had reached the site. These stones weighed upwards of two tons each – no small matter to haul them across the landscape from Wales to the Salisbury Plain. Clearly, the Neolithic people had a massive amount of skill and ambition.

New discoveries are continuously cropping up at Stone-henge and in the surrounding Salisbury Plain – which means historians and archaeologists will be puzzling over Stonehenge for years to come.

Super-Henge at Durrington Walls

A brief media frenzy occurred in 2015 at the discovery of a possible 'Super-Henge' at Durrington Walls, near Stonehenge. This circle appeared to be 500m in diameter. However, upon closer examination, the archaeologists didn't find any stones but instead found that timber posts had once stood there. Once the wooden posts had been removed, the holes had been filled with chalk, which was then covered in Earth – this formed the henge bank. On the scans of the area, the chalk had looked like stone, hence the mistake.

However, the experience provided valuable information about other undiscovered sites and features that would not have been found otherwise, including 'Woodhenge'. A massive ring of posts somewhere between 4-6 metres in height once stood in the area. At least 200, if not up to 300 such wooden posts made up the ring and would not have been discovered without the research into the potential Super-Henge.

The Great Pyramids

The Great Pyramids of Egypt, located in present-day Cairo, have long fascinated us. They dominate the landscape, with Khufu, the largest one, looming over the other two. Built in

honour of the pharaohs, for whom the ancient Egyptians held great reverence, the pyramids were part of their complex beliefs in the afterlife.

Little is known about who built the pyramids and how they managed to create such fantastic monuments constructed with such precision. Further excavation is uncovering new shafts and tunnels within the pyramids, leading archaeologists to believe that even more secrets lie within, waiting to be discovered.

Crop Circles

The mysterious phenomenon known as 'crop circles' have puzzled and delighted the public and the press alike for ages. Appearing predominately in the UK but spreading worldwide in recent decades, these elaborate patterns that appear seemingly overnight in farmers' fields have been the subject of books, films, fan groups, blogs, and their own breed of researchers called 'cereologists'. After decades of study, one question still puzzles us all: Who or what is making crop circles?

Some claim that the first documented account of a crop circle can be found in a woodcut dating from 1678, which shows a field of oat stalks flattened out in a circle. Historians say this is actually an illustration of a bit of folklore called a 'mowing devil', in which an English farmer says he 'would rather pay the Devil himself' rather than pay a worker with whom he was feuding. The devil can be seen in the image, horns and all.

Others claim the first crop circles were allegedly seen in 1966 near a small town called Tully in Australia. A farmer claimed to have seen a flying saucer rise from the land, leaving behind a flattened area in the grass. Investigators say a dust devil or waterspout most likely caused this, but the papers still referred to it as 'flying saucer nests'. As this wasn't in a crop, but was more of a circle in the grass rather than the massive designs we think of with modern crop circles, this story doesn't stand out in crop circle lore.

The first proper crop circles appeared in the English countryside in the 1970s. They were simple to start with but grew more extensive and more intricate, reaching a crescendo in the 1980s and 1990s. Some of these even illustrated complicated mathematical equations, as well as being artistically magnificent.

One of the most detailed and complex crop circles appeared near Stonehenge in 1996. The design was of a fractal pattern known as a Julia Set, a remarkably intricate piece of work that definitely could not be explained by weather phenomenon. Many believed the work to be of extra-terrestrial origin. To add to the mystery, this circle seemingly appeared in less than 90 minutes and in broad daylight. This crop circle is possibly the most well-known one to date. It was later revealed, however, that this masterpiece had, in fact, been created by three tricksters in the early hours of the morning and took three hours to complete. It wasn't spotted until later in the day by an aeroplane flying overhead.

As crop circles are real and their existence can't be denied, the argument about them is over their origin. Theories abound as to their creation, everything from wind patterns to ley lines, human artistry to horny hedgehogs (yes, you read that right). The most debated theory is if they are of alien origin, and if so, what are these aliens trying to tell us? Molecular biologist Horace Drew theorises that time travellers from the distant future cause them, and he claims to have decoded these 'messages', which are mostly warnings.

Despite all the wild theories about crop circles, only one can be proven: human creation. In 1991, two men came forward and confessed having created the circles for decades in an attempt to make people believe aliens had landed. Obviously, they didn't create all of the circles, but several copycats came forward to claim others. However, some of the circles defy logic and are impossible to attribute to human origin.

Crop circles all share a handful of characteristics. They are generally circular, with a few boasting straight or curved lines. The circles are always created at night, with a large number appearing during a full moon. No one has managed to capture their creation on camera. And lastly, they almost always appear close to main roads and are generally noticed by passing motorists shortly after their creation.

While the mystery continues and the origin of crop circles remains to be discovered, they continue to delight and astonish us with their complexity and beauty.

Nazca lines

The Nazca lines of Peru were first spotted by aircraft in the 1920s and 1930s, and they are truly astonishing to behold. Created over 2,000 years ago, the enormous designs range from simple geometric shapes to complex depictions of plants, imaginary figures, and animals. The pre-Inca Nazca people created them by removing the red pebbles on the Earth's surface, exposing the lighter soil underneath. Why they did so remains a mystery; theories abound, with ideas ranging from ancient astrology to aliens. Archaeologists are still uncertain about their use but believe they could have possibly been used in rituals to communicate with the people's gods at the time.

The Khatt Shebi

Across the landscape of Jordan lies a 93-mile-long stone wall known as the Khatt Shebi. First noticed in 1948, archaeologists are still uncertain who built it, when, or why. Running north-northeast to south-southwest, the wall comprises sections with two walls side by side and sections that branch off. Though it is now in ruins, in its prime, it would have stood nearly three and a half feet high and just over a foot and a half wide, leading archaeologists to believe it was unlikely to have been intended to protect against invaders. Instead, they think it might have been used to serve as a boundary wall between farmland and pastures, keeping livestock from wandering into neighbouring fields. Regardless, their use is uncertain, and so the mystery of the Khatt Shebi endures.

The Big Circles

Further mysteries can be found in the landscape of Jordan. Stone circles (known as the 'Big Circles'), roughly 1,300 feet in diameter and only a few feet tall, can be found strewn about the countryside. Dating back 2,000 years, eleven of these circles have been found so far, and their purpose remains a mystery. They don't have any openings, which means they wouldn't have been used to hold livestock, leaving scientists puzzled as to their use. Research continues as to the purpose of these enigmatic circles.

Curiosity has its

own reason for existence.

4. Myths and Legends

"After all, I believe that legends and myths
are rarely made of truth."

- JR Tolkein

Atlantis

Few mysteries have confounded humanity as much as the lost city of Atlantis. First appearing in the writings of the ancient Greek historian Plato in his *Republic* (c. 360 BC), this mythical island was said to be one of the great super-powers of the ancient world before a catastrophic event resulted in its sinking beneath the waves.

Supposed locations for Atlantis can be found globally: the Bahamas, Greece, Cuba, and even Japan. Historians and archaeologists also debate whether or not Atlantis actually existed or was simply a creation of Plato. Regardless, the possibility of a lost continent at the bottom of the sea has fascinated us for centuries, as can be found in books, films, TV shows, conferences, and countless blogs and websites dedicated to finding Atlantis. Without conclusive evidence, no one will ever be certain where or if Atlantis existed.

The Ark of the Covenant

According to the Book of Exodus in the Bible, the stone tablets containing the Ten Commandments were kept in a gold-encrusted wooden chest known as the Ark of the Covenant. This holy box was held in a Jewish place of wor-ship called the First Temple in Jerusalem. The Hebrew Bible says this temple was destroyed by the Babylonian army of King Nebuchadnezzar II in 587 BC, and no one has been able to locate the Ark since then. Ancient reports vary as to its location, some saying it was taken to Babylon after the sack of the city, others saying it was buried within Jerusalem, and still others saying it was destroyed along with the temple. Some modern sources claim the Ark is hidden in a monastery in Ethiopia. A recent translation of an ancient Hebrew text says the Ark will reveal itself on 'the day of the coming of the Messiah, son of David'. Until that day comes, the Ark's location remains hidden.

Noah's Ark

The famous boat from the Bible has been said to have been found multiple times in multiple locations around the world. According to the Book of Genesis in the Bible, the Ark came to rest on Mount Ararat (in what is now Turkey) after the flood. Amateur archaeologists have claimed for centuries to have found pieces of the Ark on Mount Ararat, but nothing has been proven. Naturally, researchers argue whether the Ark actually existed, and until conclusive evidence is found one way or the other, the final resting place of Noah's Ark will continue to puzzle Christians and archaeologists alike.

The Hanging Gardens of Babylon

Descriptions of a wondrous series of gardens in the ancient city of Babylon (present-day Iraq) can be found in ancient texts, dating back to around 250 BC. These 'Hanging Gardens' were said to be a wonder of the ancient world and are

described by Philo of Byzantium as having 'plants culti-
vated at a height above ground level, and the roots of the
trees are embedded in an upper terrace, rather than in the
earth.'

The remains of these fantastical ancient gardens have yet to
be discovered, leaving archaeologists to wonder, did they
ever exist? Later research has proposed that the gardens
might have actually been located in the ancient Assyrian
city of Nineveh. Unfortunately, these areas have suffered
catastrophic damage over the past two decades of war and
unrest, which means this mystery will likely remain
unsolved.

The Trojan War

Homer's epic poem *The Iliad* tells of a 10-year long war
between the Greeks (called the Achaeans) and the Trojans
called, aptly, the Trojan War. Historians are undecided as
to whether or not this ancient war was historical fact or
merely creative storytelling. The ancient Greeks claimed it
as part of their history rather than seeing it as simple fiction.

However, ancient Greek historians seem to disagree about
certain details of the war, especially as to when it took
place. Herodotus described the war as happening in the
13th century BC, meaning 800 years before his own life.
The mathematician Eratosthenes claims the war actually
took place slightly later, in 1184 BC. *The Iliad* itself shares

certain characteristics of this particular time period, such as the magnificence and size of King Priam's palace, which is reminiscent of the grand palaces of the Mycenaeans in southern Greece.

Differing accounts aside, *The Iliad* is not meant to be a historical document; it tells of a world in which men and gods alike mingled, stories of heroes and myths, taking place 400 years earlier than the world Homer lived in. Such fantasy stories of legendary heroes is surely a work of fiction…right?

The Cottingley Fairies

Over 100 years ago, the village of Cottingley in Yorkshire, England, was the source of a somewhat sensational story. Two little girls, Elsie Wright and Frances Griffiths, claimed to have taken photographs of actual fairies at the bottom of their garden. A prominent member of the Theosophical Society called Edward Gardner came across the first two photos the girls had taken, and he travelled to Yorkshire to visit the girls and prompt them to take more photos. By 1920, these photographs came to the attention of none other than Sir Arthur Conan Doyle, author of the Sherlock Holmes mysteries. He got in touch with Gardner, who by then was in possession of the infamous photos, and the two men decided to join forces to unravel the mystery of the Cottingley Fairies.

They took the photographs to various experts, some of which said the photos were authentic and could have in no way been faked, whereas others said the photos were obvious forgeries. This was enough, however, for Sir Arthur Conan Doyle, who was a great believer in fairies and desperately wanted proof of their existence. He published the photographs and an account of their discovery in the *Strand* magazine, spreading the mystery of the Cottingley Fairies far and wide.

The Cottingley Fairy photographs remain some of the most iconic fairy imagery to date, and the story has inspired books and films. Sir Arthur Conan Doyle fortunately went to his grave believing in the photos' legitimacy, as nothing had occurred to prove otherwise. Studies were carried out on the photographs up to the 1980s when the truth finally came out. In March 1983, the girls (now old women at this point) finally confessed that the photographs had been faked, and the whole thing was initially meant to be a bit of mischief that then got out of hand. However, there is one photo that Frances claimed to be genuine, and she insisted that she really did see fairies in the garden as a child. Frances stood by these claims for the rest of her life.

While the truth about the Cottingley Fairies may never fully be known, it is rather wonderful to think that magic does exist and that there may actually be more to this world than meets the eye.

The Loch Ness Monster

Loch Ness in the Scottish Highlands has long been known as the home of an elusive creature known as the 'Loch Ness Monster', or the more affectionate nickname of 'Nessie'. Loch Ness itself is rather impressive, being very long, very narrow, deeper than the North Sea, and never known to freeze over.

Sightings of Nessie go back as far as the 6th century, when an Irish saint, Saint Columba, is said to have had a run-in with the monster. The story says that St. Columba ordered one of his monks to swim across Loch Ness to retrieve a boat, already an unpleasant task even without monsters in the mix. When the monk was about halfway across the river, a roaring monster surfaced and charged at the monk. At this, Columba is said to have shouted at the beast, 'Go no further, nor touch this man! Go back!' which caused the beast to flee.

Since this exciting encounter, numerous sightings of Nessie have been reported over the years. Reports of sightings were especially prevalent in the 20th century – and these sightings were all peaceful encounters, as Nessie is never reported to have harmed anyone. This creature has, however, been great for the tourism and local business around Loch Ness! The first photograph said to be of Nessie was taken in 1933 by a surgeon from London. This photograph shows what appears to be a long neck arched over a thick body; it was published in the Daily Mail, causing quite a stir.

Another photograph was taken in 1951 by a forestry worker named Lachlan Stuart, who lived beside the loch. He saw what appeared to be three humps lined up in the water and ran to get his camera. He only managed to take one picture before the camera jammed, but the existing photograph was widely circulated as further proof of the existence of the Loch Ness Monster.

Several scientific investigations of Loch Ness have taken place over the years as interest in not only Nessie but also the Loch itself grew. The Loch Ness Phenomenon Investigation Bureau was formed in 1961, bringing in submarines and sonar experts to search the depths of Loch Ness. During one dive, one of the submarines found an enormous underwater cavern at about 950 feet deep, off the coast of Castle Urquhart – possibly the home of Nessie?

Other attempts have been made to contact Nessie. A group of four firemen, having decided that Nessie was undoubtedly a male monster, decided to make a lure to tempt Mr Nessie in 1975. They created a papier-mâché 'lady monster', complete with false eyelashes, full makeup, and a pre-recorded mating call (which was actually the mating call of a male walrus) to attract Nessie from his lair. Despite all this effort, Nessie resisted the charms of this lady monster and stayed hidden – which was a wise move on his part, as she proved rather delicate and was flattened against a jetty when caught by a sudden wind.

The most recent report of Nessie came in May 2007 from a man named Gordon Holmes, a lab technician who captured a video of a 'jet black thing, about 45 feet long, moving fairly fast in the water', in his own words. The video was broadcast on BBC Scotland and STV's *North Tonight*; however, the credibility of the video has come into question, mainly because without anything else in the shot to use as a frame of reference, the size of the 'creature' in the water can't be accurately estimated.

While reports of other monsters in other lochs around Scotland have surfaced, the Loch Ness Monster remains Scotland's most well-known and enduring mystery.

Megalodon

Otodus megalodon has officially been extinct for more than three million years, by scientific accounts at least, yet legends and rumours continue to fuel the idea that this enormous shark still survives today, living in the deepest depths of the ocean. Fossil records show that this predator, which was around 50 feet long, cruised the shallow waters near shore, feeding upon marine mammals such as whales who would come to the surface to breathe. About 3.5 million years ago, water temperatures were dropping, and the sea was undergoing drastic changes, making the marine mammals these ancient sharks preyed upon less abundant. A newly evolved competitor, the great white shark, may also have beaten the megalodon to the dwindling food sources.

However, much like with the dinosaurs, there's no conclusive evidence as to what made the meg extinct. This lack of definitive evidence has helped propagate the theory that the meg never became extinct but is, in fact living in the unexplored depths of the ocean. While scientists have used satellites to map the entirety of the ocean floor, the imagery is low-resolution and doesn't shed any light on the creatures that dwell in the deep. And while it is unlikely that this ancient creature is still alive, there is always a slight possibility. A living coelacanth, a type of fish thought to have been extinct for roughly 65 million years, turned up unexpectedly in 1938 – so there is precedent for surprises rising up from the mysterious depths of the sea.

If there was any truth to this theory, the meg would have evolved into a very different creature. Tests on the remains of other similar types of fish show that megalodon would have been warm-blooded in the same way the great white is, meaning its active cruising keeps its blood warmer than the surrounding water. This activity burns about six pounds of flesh per day for a great white, so the meg – three times the size of a great white – would have required even more food to keep it going. Fish living near the ocean floor tend to exist on scraps that rain down from above, which means the meg's metabolism would have to have dropped drastically, turning him from a cruising predator into a sluggish scavenger.

Regardless of whether or not megalodons still prowl the depths and what they look like if they actually do, the existence of this enormous shark remains one of the most fascinating legends of the deep sea.

Bigfoot

The legend of the Sasquatch, a human-like creature, has long been part of Native American tribal lore in the Pacific Northwest of the United States. However, in 1958, a construction crew in Humboldt, California, found footprints that gave new life to these stories. The prints were sixteen inches long and human-like in appearance. A local newspaper picked up the story, dubbing the mystery creature 'Bigfoot', and a new legend was born.

Another essential piece of 'evidence' came in 1967 when Roger Patterson and Bob Gimlin captured a few seconds worth of extraordinary footage where the original footprints were found. The footage, while grainy and shaky, clearly shows what appears to be a large, hairy, human-like creature, walking on two legs, turning to look at the camera before walking into the forest. This video has been highly debated in the decades since it was taken, with some insisting it's a man in a costume and others maintaining that it's legitimate.

Even though the original footprints were revealed to have been a prank perpetrated by a logger named Ray Wallace (upon his death in 2002, his children confessed it had all been intended as a joke), the legend of Bigfoot persists to this day.

El Chupacabras

Puerto Rico in the 1990s was rumoured to be infested with strange creatures. Livestock were turning up dead, drained of blood, with peculiar puncture marks on their bodies. Sightings of the culprit were reported, with descriptions varying wildly: ranging from one to two meters in height, either bipedal or quadrupedal, having a snout or a human-like mouth, etc. The name 'Chupacabras', which literally means 'goat sucker', was coined by comedian Silverio Pérez in 1995 due to the beast's predilection for draining livestock's blood, especially goats.

The Chupacabras has been spotted all over South America, as well as up into Mexico and the southern part of the United States. The most common explanation for the sightings and the livestock deaths is wild dogs or coyotes. However, others point out that dogs or coyotes would eat the livestock's flesh and wouldn't be able to drain the animals of blood. As the Chupacabras seems to be frightened away by humans, it remains to be seen if we will ever have conclusive evidence as to whether or not these creatures actually exist.

We cannot help but be in
awe when we think of the
mysteries of eternity, of life,
and of the extraordinary
structure of reality.

5. Secrets of the Deep

"The Sea is only the embodiment of a supernatural and wonderful existence."

- Jules Verne

Underwater Cairn

Scientists in Israel discovered a remarkable structure beneath the Sea of Galilee in 2003. Standing nearly 32 feet high and weighing around 60,000 tons, this structure is comprised of a number of massive stones placed atop each other. The purpose of this enormous rock pile, or 'cairn', is a puzzle. Cairns have commonly been used around the world to mark burial sites, yet none of these have been found underwater. Researchers have posed the theory that this cairn may have once been on dry land, but rising sea levels submerged it centuries ago. Researchers at the Israel Antiquities Authority believe that the cairn is more than 4,000 years old, but no conclusions have been drawn about its purpose.

Baltic Sea Anomaly

A team of divers from Ocean X made a puzzling discovery in 2011 while treasure hunting in the Baltic Sea. Their sonar showed a massive round object about 300 feet below the surface on the ocean floor. Wild theories abounded as to what it could be, including a crashed UFO or an underwater Stonehenge. Others also pointed out the resemblance to the shape of the Millennium Falcon from Star Wars. And yet others claim it could be the remains of a sunken city (Atlantis, perhaps?).

Recent research has supposedly identified the anomaly as a glacial deposit left behind when the Baltic Sea was carved out by glaciers during the Ice Age. The Ocean X team refuse to accept this explanation, claiming more mysterious things are afoot. They say that their electrical equipment all stopped working when they got within 200 metres of the object on the ocean floor, yet all switched back on when they were about 200 metres away. The Baltic Sea Anomaly remains one of the most intriguing mysteries of the sea.

Mysterious Julia Sound

'Julia' was the nickname given to an unexplained sound recorded in 1999 by the National Oceanic and Atmospheric Administration (NOAA). Lasting around 15 seconds, this spooky noise has been attributed to paranormal activity or sea monsters. The official explanation from the NOAA explains the noise is the sound of an iceberg running into the seafloor.

Bermuda Triangle

The Bermuda Triangle, located in the Atlantic Ocean off the southeastern coast of the United States, is one of the most infamous and mysterious places on the planet. Also known as the 'Devil's Triangle', this triangle between Florida, Puerto Rico, and Bermuda has been blamed for a significant number of ship and plane disappearances over the years. Christopher Colombus claims to have seen a flame crashing into the sea in this area during his first trip to the New World.

The area first came to public attention in 1918 when the USS Cyclops, a Navy ship with more than 300 people on board, disappeared without a trace in the Bermuda Triangle. In recent years, a plane with four people on board vanished from radar when it was flying to Florida from Puerto Rico. The debris of the aircraft was later found. These are just a couple of the many mishaps that have occurred in the area. Others have survived the triangle but claim their equipment stopped working when flying over the area.

Theories relating to paranormal activity or aliens have been suggested as the reason behind the disappearances and wrecks. One of the few scientific explanations proposes that a natural pull of the Earth's magnetic force redirects compasses and other equipment in the area, interfering with route planning. This, however, does nothing to explain the ships and planes that have simply vanished, never to be seen again.

Mary Celeste

The tale of the Mary Celeste is one of the most confounding maritime occurrences of recent history. On 4 December 1872, the Mary Celeste was found drifting at sea with nothing amiss and everything in its place – except the crew. Just days after it started its journey to Italy from New York, the ship was found off the coast of the Azores with no one on board and the lifeboat missing. It was discovered that nine of the barrels of raw alcohol that the ship had been transporting were missing from the hold, and a single sword was found lying on the deck. The possibility of attack by pirates has been ruled out, as everything on the ship, including the rest of the barrels as well as all the valuables belonging to the crew, were left intact.

Possible reasons have run the gamut from attack by giant squid to alien abduction, underwater earthquakes to a run-in with the aforementioned Bermuda Triangle, but none of these reasons seems to add up. This is yet another unsolved mystery of the sea, a puzzle unlikely to be solved.

Dragon's Triangle

The Pacific Ocean has its own version of the Bermuda Triangle, known as the Dragon's Triangle, located just off the coast of Japan. Magnetic anomalies, UFO sightings, and ship disappearances have all been reported in this area. In the 1950s, Japanese military vessels vanished in the area, but when researchers went in themselves to investigate, they disappeared as well. According to some historians, disappearances in this area have been recorded as far back as the Mongol Empire. Explanations have been suggested involving underwater volcanos and natural environmental changes, but the area remains a conundrum.

Michigan Triangle

Lake Michigan is one of the most impressive lakes on Earth. Spread across over 300 miles, the magnificent body of water has been linked to numerous disappearances and alien sightings in an area known as the Michigan Triangle. Dating as far back as the 19th century, multiple ships have gone missing on the lake. Captain George Donner retired to his cabin for the evening on his freighter one night in 1937, having instructed his crew to wake him when they reached their endpoint. When one of the crew went to wake him hours later, he had vanished, never to be heard from again. This mystery remains unsolved. Planes have also crashed for no apparent reason in the area. While some may say the stories have been exaggerated by conspiracy theorists, there's no doubt that strange things seem to happen around Lake Michigan.

The Franklin Expedition

HMS *Erebus* and HMS *Terror* set sail in 1845 into the Canadian Arctic with Captain Sir John Franklin at the helm and 129 men on board. Although the general assumption was that they were making an attempt to complete the North-West Passage, which connects the Atlantic to the Pacific, in actuality, their mission was to carry out a series of observations at the magnetic north pole over the winter as part of a research project. When the ships reached the north pole in September 1846, three of the men had died due to tuberculosis. Over the next 18 months, even more died – including Franklin – but the cause of death has never been determined.

In April 1848, the rest of the crew abandoned their ships, which were trapped by thick ice off King William Island. The only written record ever found of their journey is a short note explaining their intention to reach Back River, which was over 1,000 miles away. This journey was ill-advised, as they ran out of supplies and food and were unable to hunt, not to mention the hostile terrain and sub-zero temperatures. The expedition met a gruesome end, descending into cannibalism (witnessed by native hunters) and perishing less than halfway to their destination.

A number of search and rescue missions were sent from America and the UK over the following decade, and an expedition finally reached King William Island in 1859. They found the officers' final message, a boat carrying partial skeletons, and clear evidence of cannibalism. This last bit was kept secret, and a statue was erected in London to honour Franklin's supposed discovery of the North-West Passage.

The official story on what happened to the Franklin expedition was never contested until recently when Canadian archaeologists found and examined the remains of both ships. They discovered that *Terror* had journeyed south from King William Island, while *Erebus* drifted south and sank with no crew onboard to man her. Although the wrecks have been discovered, why so many men on board died and why the ships were abandoned is still an enigma.

Abu Bakr and His Fleet

In the 14th century, Emperor Abu Bakr Keita ascended the throne of Mali, a sub-Saharan African empire. Mali was one of the wealthiest African states, but Abu Bakr was ambitious to expand his kingdom. However, with the Sahara Desert and the Atlantic Ocean to either side of his empire, there was little room for expansion. In the earlier part of his reign, he funded the building of a massive armada with hundreds of ships and sent them off into the Atlantic to explore. However, only a single vessel made it back. Abu Bakr was determined and left his trusted councillor, Mansa Musa, in charge over the empire as he himself tried again. With an even grander armada of thousands of ships, Abu Bakr set off into the Atlantic with hopes of discovering new lands to conquer.

But that was the last Mansa Musa saw of Abu Bakr, as neither the Emperor nor the armada was ever seen again. Some say the Emperor founded a new empire after successfully crossing the Atlantic, but other than folk songs singing of Abu Bakr's legend, there is no proof that this ever happened.

The most spectacular reality
we can experience is the
mysterious, the source of all
true art and science.

6. Flight Disappearances

"The Guide says there is an art to flying
said Ford, or rather a knack.
The knack lies in learning how to throw
yourself at the ground and miss."

- Douglas Adams

Amelia Earhart

Already famous as the first woman to complete a solo flight across the Atlantic, Amelia Earhart became even more well-known when she disappeared without a trace in 1937. In June 1937, Earhart and her navigator, Fred Noonan, set off in their attempt to circumnavigate the globe. By July, they were on the last leg of their journey, with only the Pacific Ocean left to cross. On 2 July, heading to Howland Island in the Pacific Ocean, Earhart gave coordinates over the radio, stating that they had missed the island, and then simply said 'Wait'. Then, the transmission stopped, and she wasn't heard from again.

Despite the US navy searching the area for two weeks, neither Earhart, Noonan, nor the plane was ever found. Human remains were found on Nikumaroro, a coral reef 400 miles away from Howland Island, in 1940, but the bones were identified as belonging to a male with a shorter stature than either Earhart or Noonan. Aircraft wreckage was found on the same reef in 1991, possibly dating from the time of Earhart's disappearance, which was enough to spark public interest again.

It has also been reported by the International Group for Historic Aircraft Recovery that between 2 and 6 July 1937, fifty-seven genuine radio transmissions on Earhart's frequencies were received across North America. Most notable and rather eerie was one reported by a housewife from Texas, in which she heard Earhart reporting injuries. The search for clues has continued into recent years, yet the details of Earhart's final hours continue to prove elusive.

Flying Tiger Flight 739

Towards the beginning of the Vietnam War, US Army Flying Tiger Flight 739 disappeared on its way over the Mariana Trench in the Pacific Ocean, heading from Guam to the Philippines. Roughly one hour after the last known communication from the plane, crew on a tanker ship in the area reported seeing an explosion in the sky. Air-traffic controllers didn't receive any distress calls, making it tricky to attempt to decipher what happened on board. After an exhaustive and entirely unsuccessful search party, wild theories abounded as to what really happened to the flight. One of the favourite theories is that the plane was accidentally shot down by the United States, who then, of course, covered it up by claiming engine failure. The real reason for the plane's disappearance is unlikely ever to be discovered.

STENDEC

On 2 August 1947, a Chilean Air Force operator received a cryptic message from an airliner on its way from Buenos Aires, Argentina, to Santiago, Chile. The message from the British South American Airways Lancastrian aeroplane simply read, 'STENDEC'. This plane then went missing, never to be heard from again. Nothing was found until the 1990s, when pieces of wreckage were discovered in the Andes Mountains. In 2000, body parts were found in the same area, preserved in the ice, identified as the passengers on the missing flight.

While rumours circulated about alien abduction or Nazi attacks, a thorough investigation discovered that bad weather had caused the plane to go down, and the cryptic message was most likely based on an old World War II code standing for 'Severe Turbulence Encountered, Now Descending, Emergency Crash-landing.'

Glenn Miller over the English Channel

One of the greatest big-band leaders of all time and a legend of swing music, Glenn Miller's status as an American legend was cemented when he vanished into thin air in December 1944. He boarded a plane in London, flying out on a cold, foggy day (typical English weather) headed for Paris. However, the plane was never seen again.

The official report states that the most likely scenario was that the plane suffered from iced-over wings or engine failure and crashed into the English Channel. This theory did not satisfy the throngs of fans who mourned Glenn Miller's disappearance, and theories circulated about his fate. Some claimed he secretly landed safely yet died from cancer in a hospital a few days later, while others suggested that his plane was accidentally bombed by the English. Sadly, it seems we will never know for sure what happened to this innovator of swing.

British South American Airways *Star Tiger*

A British South American Airways Avro Tudor IV plane by the name of *Star Tiger* took off on 30 January 1948 from the Azores, the last leg of a flight to Bermuda from London. As the plane had been having problems with a heater, the aircraft was flying extremely low at 2,000 feet to keep it at a warmer temperature. It flew behind a Lancastrian plane that was serving as lookout, keeping watch for bad weather.

When this lookout plane landed successfully, ground control began to worry when the *Star Tiger* didn't immediately follow. The aircraft was never seen again, nor were any of the twenty-five passengers and six crew members on board. Despite searches and investigations, the whereabouts of the plane have never been determined, and not a single shard of glass or piece of equipment has ever been found of the *Star Tiger*.

British South American Airways *Star Ariel*

Bad luck for British South American Airways, as in January 1949, nearly one year after *Star Tiger* disappeared, another one of their flights vanished while flying from Bermuda to Jamaica. The Star Ariel noted its location in a routine communication one hour after take-off and then apparently disappeared at 18,000 feet. Due to complications, a search party was unable to set out until nearly eight hours later, giving any remains of the plane plenty of time to sink to the ocean floor.

Three common scenarios were ruled out at the time: running out of fuel, bad weather, or pilot error. It was determined that 'some external cause may (have) overwhelm(ed) both man and machine', naturally inspiring a range of conspiracy theories. Despite the theories, the most common explanation is that whatever happened, happened quickly – such as an explosion due to a defect in the plane's design. Regardless of the reason, nothing of the plane has ever been found, and all twenty passengers were reported missing and presumed dead.

Malaysia Airlines Flight MH370

The disappearance of Malaysia Airlines Flight MH370 remains the biggest aviation mystery in history. On 8 March 2014 at 12:42 am, a Malaysian Airlines Boeing 777-200ER took off from Kuala Lumpur, headed to Beijing. Onboard flight MH370 were twelve Malaysian crew members, along with 227 passengers, mostly of Chinese origin. Just before 1:30 am, as the plane reached 35,000 feet altitude and approached a waypoint near the beginning of Vietnam's air traffic jurisdiction, the pilot radioed to the controller at Kuala Lumpur Center, 'Good night. Malaysian three-seven-zero.' This was the last anyone ever heard of MH370.

The plane disappeared from radar just a few minutes later, after crossing into Vietnamese airspace. Vietnamese air controllers seeing this tried to contact the aircraft repeatedly, with no result. Military radar shows the plane veering off its original course and heading west before vanishing off military radar at 2:22 am.

What followed is the most expensive aviation search to date. Miscommunications between nations and withheld information made the search difficult, and the investigations at sea were initially concentrated in the wrong place. The Malaysian government was accused of withholding information and bungling the search efforts. After a month of fruitless searching, the focus of the investigation moved from surface waters to the ocean depths. Nothing was found until July 2015, when a piece of an aeroplane washed up on shore on the French island of Réunion. This wreckage was quickly identified as belonging to a Boeing 777, and an examination of its serial numbers showed that it had come from MH370. This confirmation of the plane's sad end put to rest any hope still held by relatives of the passengers on board. Other pieces of the aircraft have washed ashore, but the bulk of the plane is yet to be found.

Countless theories have been put forward – hijacking, computer glitch, lightning strike, mechanical failure, explosive

decompression, pilot confusion, terrorist activity, instrument failure, and so on – but none of the theories fit what little evidence has been found. All that's known for sure is that the sharp turn to the west that took the flight off course had to have been done manually, as it is too tight a turn to have been done on autopilot. Also, records of satellite communications show that the final aircraft-initiated transmission was sent at 8:19 am (Malaysia time), meaning the plane was still in the air and functioning at this time. The aircraft did not respond to a transmission sent at 9:15 am, meaning the aircraft lost the ability to communicate sometime between 8:19 and 9:15 am. Further evidence supports the theory that the plane lost control towards the end – but what remains to be found is why.

In March 2020, families of the passengers of MH370 called for further investigations in order to seek closure. A piece of a wing spoiler was found on the southern coast of South Africa in August 2020, which independent experts determined was part of MH370 and was likely torn off during an uncontrolled dive into the sea. This discovery has prompted further requests to search the ocean floor in hopes of finding evidence of what happened to MH370.

The investigation is ongoing as of May 2021.

Are we actually part of
the mystery we are
trying to solve?

7. Space and Science

"Rocket ships are exciting
but so are roses on a birthday."

- Leonard Nimoy

Black Holes

Formed when a giant star implodes into a tiny area, black holes are areas of unfathomably intense gravity, strong enough to suck light into itself. On 10th April 2019, an extraordinary development occurred where an international network of radio telescopes called the Event Horizon Telescope were able to capture a black hole and its shadow in an image for the first time. Yet, there is so much we still have to learn about this phenomenon. For example, Supermassive black holes are connected through gravity to hundreds of billions of stars but how does this relationship work? It is indeed a mystery.

The Giant Void

Rather than a hole in space, the Giant Void is precisely what it sounds like – totally empty, devoid of both matter and dark matter. Unlike a black hole, however, light can pass through the Giant Void; scientists presume it contains dark energy. While not the only such void in space, the Great Void is the largest known so far, estimated to be 1.3 billion light-years in diameter.

Dark Matter

Scientists estimate that as much as 27% of the universe is dark matter – yet dark matter remains a mystery. More is known about what dark matter is not, rather than what it is:

so far, due to the lack of light warping, we know it isn't made of black holes.

Dark Energy

As well as the supposed 27% of the universe that's made of dark matter, even more is said to be made of dark energy, which is said to make up about 68% of everything around us. (By contrast, 'normal' matter makes up only 5% of the universe.) And much like dark matter, little is known about dark energy, although the current theory is that it's behind the increasing expansion of the universe.

Saturn's mystery moon, 'Peggy'

For a short while, the planet Saturn had a mysterious little companion in the form of a moon named 'Peggy'. In 2013, NASA took a snapshot of the rings of Saturn and spotted a disturbance that astronomers believed was a little moon forming. This discovery helped scientists gain an understanding of how the sixty-seven other satellites around Saturn developed.

Sadly, as NASA pointed out in a press release regarding this little moon, 'The object is not expected to grow any larger, and may even be falling apart.' The current status of Peggy is unknown.

Is it the object that is mysterious or is it our eye that makes it mysterious?

8. Aliens and Abductions

"Two Possibilities exist: Either we are
alone in the Universe or we are not.
Both are equally terrifying."

- Arthur C. Clarke

Betty and Barney Hill

While driving home from their honeymoon in Niagara Falls in September 1961, Betty and Barney Hill were followed by a strange light. Neither of them could figure out what this light was. A few hours later when they arrived home, they both felt strange – Betty's clothes had been ripped, and Barney had strange scuff marks on his shoes – and both of their watches had stopped working. And stranger still, there were two hours of the drive that neither of them remembered.

After consulting a psychiatrist, the couple recovered some incredible memories: they said that grey men with huge eyes had led them into a silver disc-shaped craft the size of a house, did examinations on them, then erased their memories. This revelation led to government investigation and was the first widely publicised account of alien abduction. No conclusion has ever been reached about what really happened that night in 1961.

Travis Walton

One night in 1975, a man named Travis Walton was working in Snowflake, Arizona as a forestry worker, along with several of his friends. The men saw what they claimed to be a strange craft in the sky, and while the rest of them fled, Walton was knocked unconscious. When the others came back to look for him, Walton had vanished, and he didn't turn up for another five days. Upon his return, he claimed he'd been abducted by aliens as well as alien/human hybrids.

Walton has stuck with this story over the years and has undergone various lie detector tests. To make things more confusing, he passed some of the tests but failed others. No conclusion has ever been reached about what really happened to Walton. However, his story caught the interest of Hollywood, and the film *Fire in the Sky* is based on his tale.

Meng Zhaoguo Incident

A man named Meng Zhaogua was walking through the Red Flag Forest of Heilongjiang in China in 1994. He says that he and a relative had been following a strange object in the sky, which he claims to have watched descend. After the craft landed, the aliens on board captured Meng Zhaoguo and forced him to have sex with them. He claims they showed him Mars and that they said it was their home.

UFO communities in China have differing opinions on this story. Some believe that he was captured but doubt his claims about what happened afterwards. We will most likely never know the truth of these claims.

Pascagoula Abduction

Co-workers Charles Hickinson and Calvin Parker claim that while they were on a fishing trip in 1973, they were taken by aliens. These two said they were conscious for the abduction and that while they were fishing, two flashing blue lights appeared, and they heard a strange noise before a large object appeared hovering over them. The creatures that supposedly took them had 'robotic slit mouths' and 'crab-like pincers' and examined the pair after taking them on board the craft. Similar to most alien abduction stories, opinion is divided as to whether or not this terrifying encounter actually occurred.

Matlock Triangle

In the Derbyshire Dales is an area known as the 'Matlock Triangle'. This area has been called the UFO capital of the world. Stories abound of strange, glowing objects flying over the countryside, in a variety of shapes ranging from cylindrical aircraft to one described as 'like a bowler hat'.

One of the more well-known sightings was made by a self-proclaimed 'complete and utter disbeliever' named Sharon Rowlands, who saw a huge, colourful disc hovering in the air over her village. Rowlands managed to capture the incident on her camcorder and sold the footage to an American TV company for a tidy sum of money.

Similar to the Bermuda Triangle, opinion varies on whether the stories of alien sightings over this area are tall tales or genuine.

Bridgewater Triangle

Yet another triangle, the Bridgewater Triangle of Massachusetts is a fearsome landscape. Thick forests and bleak wetlands cover the area, which is very easy to get lost in. This area is home to one of the very first sightings of a UFO, dating back to 1760 when witnesses described a 'sphere of fire' bright enough to be seen across multiple towns.

While travelling in a carriage in 1908, a pair of undertakers claim to have seen a flying object which they described as being like 'an unusually strong lantern'. Their story was backed up by other witnesses, some of which assumed it had been a hot air balloon. The undertakers disagreed, saying, 'I claim that a hot air balloon could not move in a circle or perpendicular as this one did.'

Wild stories of strange phenomenon have been told of the area since then, everything from tales of strange creatures in the forest to massive flying monsters in the sky. Livestock have also been mutilated in the area, with no explanation. Whether or not the area is home to strange creatures and frequented by UFOs remains a mystery.

Is it much more intriguing
to live not knowing than
to have answers that
might be wrong?

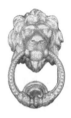

9. Missing Persons and Unsolved Crimes

"The most loving parents and relatives
commit murder with smiles on their faces.
They force us to destroy the person we
really are: a subtle kind of murder."

- Jim Morrison

Disappearance of the Sanxingdui

While making repairs to a sewage ditch in the Sichuan province of China, a man discovered a hoard of jade and stone artefacts in 1929. These beautiful treasures made their way into private collections. In 1986, archaeologists uncovered two more troves full of items dating from the Bronze Age; these included elephant tusks, bronze sculptures, and more jade.

However, no one could figure out who had hidden these treasures. After further research, archaeologists concluded that these artefacts came from the Sanxingdui civilisation, which collapsed between 3,000 and 2,800 years ago. The Sanxingdui once lived in a walled city on the banks of the Minjiang River. The mystery lies in why they hid these items before leaving the city. In 2014, researchers suggested that the inhabitants may have been forced to move when an earthquake 3,000 years ago rerouted the city's river. Research continues to discover why the Sanxingdui fled their home and left their treasures behind.

The Lost Maya

The vibrant Mayan civilisation collapsed around AD 900, but the reason for the downfall remains unclear. Archaeologists in Mexico and Central America have been trying to solve this mystery for decades.

Some suggest that a drought may have been the undoing of the Mayans, as they cleared forests to make room for more cities and farmland, which would have worsened any drought. Other theories point towards soil degradation and the decline of wild food sources, while still others claim shifting trade routes and political conflict may have led to their demise. The collapse of the Mayans remains one of the biggest global mysteries to date.

The Ninth Legion

For centuries, historians have puzzled over the disappearance of the Ninth Legion. The Legion was one of four elite military units occupying Britain after the Romans invaded in AD 43. The Legion was rebuilding the fortress of York in AD 108, according to the records, but they simply vanished twelve years later, and their name was absent from all following military lists.

One of the more popular theories is that the 5,000 soldiers of the Legion marched north to deal with a rebellion but were taken by surprise and killed in Caledonia. This theory has been the subject of *The Eagle of the Ninth* by Rosemary Sutcliffe, as well as the films *Centurion* and *The Eagle*.

In recent years, however, historians have challenged this theory, saying the Ninth was more likely transferred and killed somewhere in the eastern reaches of the Roman empire, yet no solid evidence exists to support this hypothesis. An inscription on the Fortress Gate in York, which includes the titles of Emperor Trajan, dates to AD 108, showing the Ninth were there around this time. Whereas the only evidence to support a transfer to the east is a few bits of pottery, a pendant, and some shards of tile bearing the mark of the Ninth, found in the Netherlands. While this does show that the Ninth or part of it was sent to this area, they seem to be from the early AD 80s.

In the AD 160s, the roman historian Fronto wrote that in the absence of Emperor Hadrian, the British slew large numbers of Roman soldiers. It was also noted that 'The Britons could not be kept under Roman control', implying that the natives were fighting back against Rome. Records show that emergency reinforcements were sent to Britain early during Hadrian's reign. Hadrian himself even came to the area and took up residence in the former base of the Ninth, implying that trouble in the area was prevalent.

While evidence seems to point to their annihilation by the Britons, any theories on the final fate of the Ninth Legion will remain speculation until further evidence is discovered.

Roanoke Island

In July 1585, Sir Richard Grenville landed at Roanoke Island with 600 men. Roanoke, an island off what would later be known as North Carolina, was inhabited by the indigenous Secotans, yet instead of making allies of the tribe, the governor of the new colony, Ralph Lane, treated them brutally. This meant that when his settlers ran low on food, rather than being able to turn to the natives for help, Grenville had to return to England to bring back supplies. In Grenville's absence, Lane grew suspicious of the natives and led an attack that massacred many of them, including their Chief, Wingina. While the Secotans were defeated, the colony was left in shambles. Sir Francis Drake rescued the surviving settlers two weeks later, including Governor Lane. Grenville returned in the summer of 1586 briefly before leaving again.

A new group of settlers returned to Roanoke in May 1587, led by John White, one of the original settlers. His pregnant daughter, Eleanor Dare, went with him. White did not have a flair for leadership, and once again, the settlers failed to establish a good relationship with the local natives. Therefore, another trip back to England for supplies was necessary, and White said goodbye to his daughter and his new granddaughter, Virginia Dare (the first child born to English parents in America).

White was delayed in returning to Roanoke until 18 August 1590, which was Virginia Dare's third birthday. But upon his return, not only Virginia but the entire colony had vanished, all 115 of them. White's house was in disarray, and his possessions scattered around, but there was no sign of the settlers, no graves, no bones. What they did find was the word 'Croatoan' carved into the palisade. As this was the name of an island fifty miles to the south, White hoped his family had sailed there, but he didn't have time to investigate, as hurricane season forced him to sail back to Plymouth.

Any search expeditions came back empty-handed. A report from the Powhatan tribe reached London in 1609, saying the Roanoke settlers had been killed, but there was no evidence to back this up. Hundreds of years later, in the early 18th century, visitors to Hatteras Island (what Croatoan was known as by then) encountered what they thought to be evidence of the English. Old stories surfaced of light-eyed, light-skinned indigenous children, which suggested the assimilation of the original settlers or Roanoke. There's no way to know for sure, as DNA analysis requires bones or living relatives, and the more common belief is that the pale indigenous children had a form of albinism.

Even the exact location of Roanoke is unknown. The site is now most likely underwater due to coastal erosion, and this theory was bolstered when a swimmer found a 16th-century axe head in the area in 2002.

In 2011, researchers discovered a drawing of a fort beneath a patch on a map by John White. Archaeologists found Elizabethan artefacts at this site in 2017, fifty miles west of Roanoke, but it's unclear if these artefacts belonged to the original colonists. Theories about the fate of the colonists of Roanoke are plentiful: enslavement by the Spanish, relocation to one of Sir Walter Raleigh's secret operations, resettlement in Chesapeake Bay, or shipwreck. A grave marker inscribed by Eleanor Dare was found in 1937 in a North Carolina swamp but dismissed to be a forgery. Yet some are now beginning to wonder if it was authentic after all. The only thing that is certain about the mystery of Roanoke is that it will continue to puzzle historians until it's solved.

Jack the Ripper

A terror stalked the streets of London in 1888, a man named Jack the Ripper. The mutilated bodies of five women were found, all murdered. The Ripper sent letters to the police, taunting them and challenging them to find him. (The authenticity of these letters is still a topic of debate among historians.) Despite the best efforts of the police, the Ripper was never found, and dozens of people have been suggested as possible candidates in the years since. A woman named Lizzie Williams was suggested to be the Ripper in a recent book, but other experts doubt this theory. Unfortunately, the identity of the Ripper may never be known for sure.

Jimmy Hoffa

On 30 July 1975, a teamster union leader named Jimmy Hoffa disappeared from Oakland County, Michigan. Hoffa

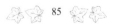

was known to be involved with organised crime, but the reason for his disappearance isn't known. He is now presumed to be dead, but his body has never been found, despite searches of a number of sites in Oakland and Detroit by forensic anthropologists and police.

A popular theory was that Hoffa was buried in New Jersey beneath Giants Stadium, but this has been debunked.

In 2006, a hitman named Richard 'The Iceman' Kuklinski claimed to have dumped Hoffa's body in a scrap yard after killing him. Kuklinski died shortly after this confession, and doubt was cast on his confessions by police officers in media interviews. Author Philip Carlo wrote a book based on Kuklinski's confessions after visiting him in prison before his death, but it's uncertain if there is any truth to the story. It's now doubted that Hoffa's body and the way he died will ever be discovered.

JFK

The assassination of President John F. Kennedy is probably the most enduring mystery in American history. Lee Harvey Oswald shot Kennedy on 22 November 1963, although it's speculated that he didn't' act alone. Before Oswald could stand trial, he was shot and killed by nightclub owner Jack Ruby on 24 November 1963. Ruby himself died of lung cancer in January 1967.

The most commonly accepted theory is that after Oswald killed JFK, Ruby killed Oswald. Ruby stated that his motivation was to spare Jacqueline Kennedy from the discomfort of Oswald standing trial. Despite this theory, a large number of amateurs and professional historians alike do not accept this explanation, and numerous alternative theories have been proposed. As new evidence is likely to never be found, the public will probably never agree on the circumstances surrounding JFK's death.

Agatha Christie

Agatha Christie, the 'Queen of Crime' herself, was the subject of a mystery worthy of one of her own books in 1926. On 3 December, Christie had an argument with her husband, Archie, who had asked her for a divorce. She then kissed her seven-year-old daughter goodnight, got into her car (a Morris Cowley) and vanished.

A media field day ensued. A thousand police officers were deployed to search for her. Dorothy L Sayers, Christie's rival, searched for clues in the house, and Sir Arthur Conan Doyle himself consulted a medium for information regarding Christie's whereabouts. A headline on the front page of the *Daily Express* read, 'Clues in the Riddle of Mrs Christie – Hatless Woman Met on the Downs – 5 am Incident – Helped by a Man to Start Her Car.' The mystery could have been written by Christie herself, as thrilling as puzzling as it was.

The search continued for ten days until Christie was discovered in the Swan Hydro Hotel in Harrogate on 14 December. She had checked in under a false name and had taken part in the hotel's activities for days until she was recognised when she claimed to have lost her memory. Even more curious still was the name she used to check in. Her husband had been having an affair with a woman whose surname was Neele, and this is the name Christie had used.

Doctors corroborated Christie's insistence that she'd lost her memory, even while people suspected it was a publicity stunt. Some think she staged the whole event to humiliate her cheating husband; others say she most likely suffered from a nervous breakdown. The truth will never be known, as Christie herself never talked about the incident again, even in her autobiography. Her fans will never know the truth of Agatha Christie's most enduring mystery.

Bennington Triangle

The Bennington Triangle, which comprises Glastenbury Mountain and the surrounding ghost towns of Vermont, has been the eerie setting for several disappearances. A local man named Middie Rivers led a group of hikers near the mountain in 1945. As he was walking ahead of the group, he seemed to vanish into thin air. The following year, a teenager named Paula Welden disappeared while hiking in the same area. A media storm followed, and massive searches took place, but they found nothing. A child named Paul Jepson was waiting in his mother's car some years later while she visited an area near the mountain, yet when she returned to the car, the boy had vanished. Hundreds of volunteers searched the area with no result.

As both Middie and Paul were wearing red clothes at the times of the disappearances, a superstition has arisen that wearing red to visit Glastenbury Mountain is bad luck. UFOs have also been seen in the area, and others have vanished as well, making this a morbid tourist destination for paranormal investigators and anyone with a fascination for the unexplained.

Mystery exists at the
very heart of creativity.

10. Future Predictions

"The future belongs to those who believe in the beauty of their dreams."

- Eleanor Roosevelt

Nostradamus

The prophecies of the 16th-century seer and apothecary Michel de Nostredame are the stuff of legend. Nostradamus is said to have predicted major world events occurring over four centuries after his death. One of the most well-known is about the Great Fire of London, which ravaged the city in 1666. Writing in his book *Les Propheties* in 1555, he said, 'The blood of the just will be lacking in London, burnt up in the fire of' 66.'

Nostradamus also seems to have predicted the French Revolution of 1789. He wrote: 'From the enslaved populace, songs, chants and demands, while princes and lords are held captive in prisons.' This sounds strikingly like the uprising of the peasants and arresting of the French aristocracy during the Revolution. He also wrote of 'headless idiots', which has been theorised to refer to the execution of thousands of people by guillotine, including King Louis XVI and Maria Antoinette, during the Reign of Terror.

It has been said that it's best to remain objective while studying the prophecies of Nostradamus, as his writings were so prolific that you could potentially find predictions for just about anything contained within his work. The similarities to the events listed above, as well as many others within his writing, are so striking, however, that it does make you wonder.

E.M. Forster

E.M. Forster wrote of a world in which life is conducted in people's own rooms, and they communicate with each other solely through electronic means. In this book, The Machine Stops, he describes how people use these electronic communications to form friendships, groups, and teams and eventually become phobic of the outside world and meeting people in person. Keep in mind, at this point in time, the radio was virtually unknown; the telephone and television did not exist. Did he predict a world in which humans spend more time on the internet and social media than outdoors?

Morgan Robertson

In *The Wreck of the Titan*, Morgan Robertson wrote of an enormous passenger ship called *The Titan*, which sank in the freezing Atlantic Ocean, killing thousands after hitting an iceberg. The ship was described as 'the largest ship of its time' yet suffered from a shortage of lifeboats. *The Titan* was named 'unsinkable'.

Does any of this sound familiar? The mystery lies in the original publishing date of this novella: originally called *Futility*, this story was published in 1898, 14 years before *Titanic* sank beneath the waves.

Mark Twain

Legend of American literature Mark Twain predicted the timing of his own death in his 1909 autobiography. Twain was born in November 1835, shortly after Halley's comet had become visible from Earth, which it does around every 75 years. At age 74, Twain wrote: 'I came in with Halley's comet in 1835. It is coming again next year, and I expect to go out with it.' And, true to his prediction, Twain died the very next day after the comet appeared again in April 1910.

Edgar Cayce

In the early 1920s, a man named Edgar Cayce became famous for his mystic powers. He would go into a trance and answer questions on any subject, ranging from personal issues to affairs of state. His most well-known clients were Thomas Edison and Woodrow Wilson. Cayce began warning people in 1925 that a catastrophic economic depression would sweep across America in 1929. His savvier clients listened to him and withdrew their savings from banks, and they were lucky they listened to him. Sure enough, as predicted, the New York Stock Exchange crashed in 1929, plunging millions of people into unemployment and creating one of the worst economic depressions America has ever seen, lasting until 1954.

Cayce's prophecies were prolific. He predicted in 1938 that archaeologists would discover in 1968 or 1969 under 'the slime of ages and sea water near Bimini' (in the Bahamas) something to represent 'the rising of Atlantis'. In 1968, the Bimini Road was discovered; this is a mysterious underwater rock formation resembling a road, which many claim to be evidence of the lost city of Atlantis.

Cayce's final prediction was accurate as well: On 1 January 1945, he prophesied that he would be buried in four days. Accurate until the end, on 3 January, he died of a stroke.

The Simpsons

Besides being one of the most beloved and longest-running television shows of all time, *The Simpsons* seems to have accurately predicted future events on several occasions. Here are just a few:

In 1990, Bart catches a three-eyed fish in a river near the nuclear power plant his father, Homer, works at. Over ten years later, a three-eyed fish was found in Argentina in a reservoir fed by water from a local nuclear power plant.

A 1991 episode featured Ringo Starr answering fan mail from decades earlier. In 2013, Paul McCartney sent a reply to a letter and a recording from two fans in Essex – which had been written and sent to The Beatles fifty years prior.

During a live performance in 2003, one of Siegfried and Roy's white tigers, named Montecore, attacked Roy on

stage. Roy survived but sustained severe injuries. This in itself probably isn't that strange, but what is odd is that the scenario had already played itself out in an episode of *The Simpsons* in 1993. In the episode, a trained white tiger mauls the magicians while they're performing in a casino.

In a 1994 episode, two school bullies type 'beat up Martin' into a Newton device, the iPhone's ancient ancestor. The device translates the memo to read 'eat up Martha'. Could this be a foreshadowing of autocorrect?

'Lisa's Wedding' episode, airing in 1995, showed a number of predictions for the future, but one stands out. When Lisa travels to London, a building is visible on the skyline behind Tower Bridge that looks remarkably like The Shard. Construction on The Shard started fourteen years later. Did the episode inspire the design for the building, or was this a case of another eerily accurate prediction?

A 1998 episode shows Homer becoming an inventor, and he's shown standing in front of a complex equation on a blackboard. Author Simon Singh says this equation predicts the mass of the Higgs boson particle, which was predicted in 1964 but wasn't confirmed until 2013 when proof was discovered in an experiment costing 10.4 billion pounds.

In 'When You Dish Upon a Star', an episode that aired in 1998, Homer pitches a script that gets picked up and produced by 20th Century Fox. In front of the studio's headquarters is a sign that says 'a division of the Walt Disney Company'. Nearly twenty years later, Disney purchased 21st Century Fox and acquired 20th Century Fox (the film studio) as part of the deal.

In a 2012 episode, Lady Gaga hangs in midair during a performance for the town of Springfield. Five years after this, Gaga performed her Super Bowl halftime show which featured her hanging in the air.

Is time the greatest

mystery of all?

Conclusion

So are you surprised by the number of things we don't know?

So many of us are focused on knowing everything. While there is nothing wrong with the pursuit of knowledge, learning, and understanding, our burning desire to know and control all that is around us can get in the way of trying new things, exploring different ways, accomplishing new feets and thereby becoming more satisfied and at peace with ourselves

Imagine if we could let go, trust, and be at peace with not knowing? Being able to embrace not knowing is arguably one of the most important, yet challenging aspects of truly appreciating life and really growing as a person. Being at peace with not knowing allows us to be creative, open, and happy to be in a state of wonder and possibility.

When we accept that we don't know, we can:

1) Relax - Take our hands off the controls and trust that we don't have to do and know everything in order to succeed and be happy and be appreciated. When we release these things, an inner peace and freedom can show up very naturally.

2) Stop pretending that we know everything. It is stressful, often annoying to others, and self defeating. We aren't supposed to know or understand everything and neither are we expected to think that we do. The more we can admit we don't know something, the more likely we are to be able to discover it, learn about it, let it go if needs be, ask for assistance, and be happy about it.

3) Be more inquisitive - Looking for things and embracing things that we don't understand, know about, or think we can do. All this boosts our confidence, encourages us to expand ourselves, and gives us practice at being comfortable in the unknown and uncertain ways of life.

This is arguably where the most important growth, transformation and new opportunities can occur.

Strangely not knowing puts us on the path to really knowing, but we have to leave space for the not knowing otherwise the real knowing will never come.

Many many new thoughts, ideas and inventions will come in the next decades and the best way to prepare for, initiate and accelerate that is to be in the space of the unknown.

In 1889, Charles H Duell who was the Commissioner of the US Patent Office stated that the Patent Office would soon shrink in size and eventually close, because..."Everything that can be invented has been invented." Let's not make that mistake today. However, it is not just to do with what can be invented but what can be or can ever be created in our lives and in the lives of those around us.

Where does our journey begin and end? Most of it resides unquestionably in the unknown.

Let's embrace that!

About the Author

James Sanderson is an Entrepreneur based in London with a particular passion for Networking and Empowering People across the World.

He travels and speaks extensively and with such a diverse number of activities is affectionately known as

The International Man Of Mystery

www.sandersonselect.com
james@sandersonselect.co.uk